How to write flexible learning materials

A brief practical guide

Roger Lewis

NCET
National Council for Educational Technology

Published in 1990 by NCET
National Council for Educational Technology
Sir William Lyons Road
Science Park
University of Warwick
Coventry CV4 7EZ

ISBN 1 85379 117 2

Contents

Acknowledgements

This book owes much to participants in the many writing workshops I have run or been involved in since about 1975. I am very grateful to the many people from industry, colleges, training schemes, voluntary bodies and higher education who have applied themselves to the challenge of writing material for use in open and flexible learning.

A draft of this book was sent for detailed comment to four colleagues across the spectrum of industry, schools and higher education. I acknowledge their help: Avrille Close, Yvonne Jeffries, Peter Kay and John Lougher. I should also like to thank Peter Kay for his additional help on the Design and Production sections.

My colleague, Claire Bradley, educates me continuously on desk-top publishing.

Chris Bailey helped me with the illustrations and I am particularly grateful to Una Crumpton for her support in presenting the manuscript.

Any errors you find are my own responsibility.

1. Introduction

Who is this book for?

This book is aimed at anyone responsible for education and training – lecturers, teachers, trainers – whether in industry, the public education sector or in voluntary organisations. You could, for example, be involved in a Training Agency initiative, such as Employment Training, the Flexible Learning Project in Schools, Enterprise in Higher Education (or their successors).

You want:

- to put together a short unit of printed material for use in flexible or open learning schemes ('short' means roughly of one hour's learning time – you could, of course, add together several such units to form a course)

- to use unsophisticated production technology (for example a bottom-of-the-range Amstrad) with no back-up (editors, designers etc.). You want to produce the material yourself without sub-contracting to other people or using a long and complex production chain. You may, though, have an individual working with you, for example inputting and designing your materials, and you may have access to occasional help from a media resources unit (for example in a school or polytechnic)

- to use the material with a learner or group of learners in a supported situation, i.e. with a tutor, lecturer or trainer available for at least some of the time when the material is being used.

I assume that you have on hand a friend, or colleague, who will read what you write and comment, and some learners on whom you can try out your ideas and materials.

What does the book help you to do?

The book helps you to create the materials, that is, to write:

- objectives so your learners can see clearly what they have to achieve
- questions and activities so your learners can achieve their objectives
- feedback to give your learners evidence on how well they're doing
- linking text.

It also helps you to:

- plan the design of your materials, including any illustrations
- take the material through the necessary production stages
- plan and run a pilot version to get feedback on the effectiveness of your unit so you can amend it
- monitor your unit in use and update it as necessary.

The section on scheduling will help you to see how long all this might take and to draw up your own timetable.

The book covers all the production stages, from writing through to monitoring the use of the finished product. It restricts itself to print; this is by far the most common and practicable medium for most people to use. The book includes a note on audio tape but it does not discuss other more complex and expensive media such as interactive video. Use of these means assembling and managing a team, including specialists (not to mention a substantial budget!). An annotated resources list points you to wider or more advanced help.

What else will the book help you achieve?

The book covers writing flexible learning materials. But in the process you will develop many other related skills such as:

- curriculum design and planning
- setting learning objectives
- evaluation.

You need all these for flexible learning. But you also need them for other forms of learning delivery. For some readers the major benefit of working through this book will be that they improve their *existing* delivery methods, whether in classroom, seminar room or training centre.

What prior experience does the book assume?

Before you sit down to write learning material there are a number of activities you need to have carried out. You need to have:

- decided that there is a real need for your material and that nothing suitable already exists
- worked out who will use your material and under what circumstances (you will need to think of your users throughout)
- decided that print is a suitable medium for learning.

If you need further help on these four decisions see the section on Planning in the Resources List.

You will also need to have:

- broken down the learning area into manageable chunks
- worked out routes learners might take through these chunks, according to their ability or purpose.

If you need further help with these two processes, you will find other sources in the Resources List.

It is also assumed that you have access to, and can use, a word-processing system – or that you have a colleague to do your word processing for you.

What are the features of the book?

I try throughout to keep the treatment simple. There is nothing inherently difficult about producing text for use in flexible and open learning. It's more a matter of extending your existing skills and learning one or two new ones.

Most of the sections are illustrated with examples. These are shown by EG. The examples are mostly taken from workshops I have run to help people from mixed backgrounds (industry, the health service, schools, voluntary bodies and higher education). The examples are deliberately simple and general. This means that you can see the essential principles in action, uncomplicated by technical background.

Each section begins with an objective O and a note on the importance of the stage covered I. Under I you will also find a summary of what is covered in the section.

Brief checklists help you focus on essential points; these are shown CL.

A Glossary defines key terms and the Resources List will guide you to other sources of help.

What approach does the book take?

The book is meant for immediate practical use, directly to produce material. Throughout it recommends that you follow these stages:

- Try out the activity (for example write the objectives, suggest an idea for an illustration) and review your work using the checklists provided.

- Get your friend/colleague and the learner(s) to comment on what you've produced. They too, can use the relevant checklists to do this.

- Think about the feedback you get and revise your work accordingly.

The cyclical process is very important: progress will be achieved by constant redrafting. So make sure you set up some friendly commentators on your work. You may even choose to draft with a collaborator, alternately writing and commenting on one another's work. Peer support is very important.

You are reminded of the importance of the draft/comment/redraft cycle by the icon [↻].

Further practice

Writing is a skill you develop with practice. It is, by definition, a lonely activity, but you can gain a lot by discussing with other people what you write. That's why I so strongly recommend your involving a friend, and learners, in your work. An extension of this is to attend a writing workshop. In that way, you will meet other people in the same position and get wider feedback on your work. NCET, NEC and the OC run such workshops and their addresses are given in the Resources List. Your local polytechnic or teachers' centre may also be able to organise writing workshops.

Accreditation in writing and production

The Certificate in Open Learning Delivery means you can now get formal credit and public recognition for writing and producing flexible learning materials. For details of how to do this contact Training Development Services, The Open College, St James's Building, Oxford Street, Manchester M1 6FQ.

Key to icons used

[O] the objective of a section, i.e. what it helps you do

[I] why this section is important

CL checklists: summary of key action points

EG example

↻ a reminder to follow the cyclical process: do it/get comments on it/change it as necessary.

Terms

The Glossary explains all key terms but you should note three in particular:

- 'Learner' is used to describe the end user of the unit, whether student in a college or university, trainee in a government scheme, employee in a company or pupil in a school.
- 'Supporter' is the person who helps learners use the unit, whether professional (the 'tutor') or non-professional (e.g. a friend, member of the family or a colleague).
- 'Unit' describes the learning material this book helps you to produce, i.e. material occupying about one hour of learner time.

2. Objectives

[O] This section helps you write objectives for your unit.

[I] Your unit is intended to bring about learning. This means that you want to help learners change in some way. It might be a change:

- in knowledge; learners know more or can do new things with their knowledge
- in skill; learners can carry out a new practical operation, or improve an existing skill
- in attitudes; learners feel – for example – more confident, more enthusiastic, more assertive or more sympathetic.

Or the change could include all these ingredients, combined.

Writing objectives will be useful both to you and to learners. It helps *you* become clear about what change you hope will result from the learner interacting with your unit. More important, objectives help *learners* see immediately what they can expect to learn from the unit; i.e. what the pay-off, or benefit, will be to them.

This section distinguishes 'objectives' from 'aims' and then suggests an approach to writing objectives.

Aims and objectives

Aims and objectives are often confused. Aims are intentions; for example, a biology teacher's aim could be 'to cover digestion next term'. Objectives, on the other hand, are detailed statements of what learners will achieve, or how their behaviour will change as a result of learning. Thus objectives are statements of learner behaviour – 'list the mains steps of digestion . . . label a diagram to show how digestion takes place'.

The verb

Objectives should always be couched in terms of what the learner will do. So, at the minimum, objectives should begin with a verb that clearly indicates learner behaviour – as in the following examples, from a unit designed to help young children maintain their bicycles.

> EG This unit will help you:
>
> - check your cycle visually for safety defects
> - test the brakes on your cycle
> - adjust the brakes so they work effectively
> - fit new brake blocks.

In the above example the outcome is immediate and practical. Sometimes the 'doing' will be mental and lead to an output such as a list, definitions of terms, the correct completion of a wiring diagram or a calculation. In all cases, though, the author should state clearly the anticipated learner behaviour.

An additional benefit of using a behavioural verb is that it leads directly to an assessment check. When you look at an objective it will immediately suggest how learners' progress towards reaching it can be assessed.

Conditions and standards

Sometimes objectives need to include more than just the verb. In industrial training they may also need to spell out the conditions in which learners' behaviour should occur and/or the standards learners should achieve – how well they must perform the task – as in the example below.

> EG Carry out (*verb*) all safety checks listed in the unit (*standard*) without reference to any notes (*conditions*).

How many objectives?

For a one-hour learning period you would normally use only one to two objectives.

Summary

Figure 1 below sets out the main points to remember when writing objectives.

STRONG	EXAMPLE	WEAK	EXAMPLE
Describes learner behaviour	You will be able to adjust your brakes	Describes teacher behaviour	I shall cover the ways in which brakes are adjusted
Describes behaviour	You will adjust brakes	Describes subject matter	The adjustment of brakes
Describes observable behaviour	List, label, sort, adjust	Describes states of mind	Know, understand, appreciate
Each objective describes one outcome only	1. test your brakes 2. adjust your brakes	Each objective describes several outcomes	Test your brakes and adjust them if necessary
Are concise	Adjust your brakes	Are wordy	Carry out all necessary adjustments to the braking system employed on your bicycle

Fig. 1: Writing objectives – strong and weak points, with examples

CL Use the left-hand column of Figure 1 to check the objectives you have written. Amend them as necessary.

Don't forget to let others comment on your objectives. Can you phrase them more simply and clearly?

3. Assessment

O — This section helps you to write questions, activities, assignments – and other means by which learners can assess their progress.

I — This stage follows logically from the previous one. You now need to help learners work out how far they are meeting the objectives you have set. If your objectives are sound it will be easy to design means of testing their achievement. But you also need to make the tests interesting and varied and this is what the section concentrates on.

Three main types of test are covered:

- Self-completion tests; questions that learners answer and check for themselves, using information given in the unit.
- Activities; these encourage learners to apply their learning to the world outside the unit.
- Assignment; work completed by learners and passed or sent to a tutor for assessment.

The timing of the test will vary. Self-completion tests can, for example, be set both within the unit and at the end, thus giving learners two chances to check their grasp of content. Assignments will often be placed at the end of a unit, or even of a group of units. Activities could appear anywhere.

Each type of test should complement the others. Self-completion tests could, for example, arm the learner with information needed to carry out an activity; the activity could form a stepping-stone to an assignment sent for tutor assessment.

This section looks briefly at each type of assessment test. More information on testing can be found in the Appendix and in the Resources List.

Self-completion tests

This type of assessment is self-contained, that is, everything is provided within the unit to enable learners to check their own understanding of material. The process is simple:

- you set a question in the unit and stimulate the learner to respond
- the learner responds, often by writing in a space provided in the test itself
- you provide feedback, either immediately following the question or elsewhere in the unit
- learners compare their responses to yours.

Writing feedback to tests is covered in more detail in the next section.

Self-completion tests have a number of functions. They can be used to arouse interest in what is to come, for example, by asking learners what they already know about a new topic. More commonly, though, they check mastery of material that has already been covered in the unit.

Such questions are often set in two places: within and at the end of the unit. This gives learners two chances to check progress. Questions at the end of a unit can also test learners' ability to integrate material included in various sub-sections.

When in the text, these tests are often called 'self-assessment questions'; other names include 'self-check', 'self-test'. When at the end of a unit they may be called 'review questions', 'end tests', 'check your learning' (or a similar term). Questions should be appropriate and should not introduce unnecessary difficulty.

> EG If the objective required learners to connect two parts of a diagram, this is what the test should ask them to do. To ask learners to describe the process in words would be both inappropriate and too difficult.

Some of the main types of self-completion test are shown in the Appendix.

Activities

Activities require learners to transfer learning from the unit and

- relate it to their own experience
- apply their learning to the real world.

EG Follow the financial pages over the next week. Note any announcement (government policy, inflation etc.) and see the extent to which the share prices are affected.

EG For an example of an action plan see the Scheduling section of this book.

EG Find a safe place to cycle. Ride the bicycle a short way then stop. Can you touch the ground easily? If not, you will need to adjust the saddle to a lower position.

Activities may involve a third person, as in the example below.

EG Now give the presentation to your colleague. Ask your colleague to complete the following checklist. Then ask him or her to give you feedback on your strengths and weaknesses.

EG Carry out the following tests. They will help you make sure the bearings are are adjusted correctly. Ask your partner to watch you make the tests. Give them the pink sheet, which tells them exactly what to look for.

Activities are often accompanied by checklists. These are particularly useful for practical skills and for skills requiring interaction between people, for example interviewing or working as part of a team. Checklists can be used not only by learners themselves, but also by supporters watching or guiding them, and by assessors.

EG See the checklists in this book.

Assignments

An assignment requires learners to submit work to a tutor for comment and assessment. The presence of a professional assessor is what distinguishes an 'assignment' from an 'activity'. The boundaries are not always exact, for example the results of an activity could become part of an assignment.

Assignments can be within the unit or separate. The advantages and disadvantages of the alternatives are set out in Figure 2.

Assignments should make good use of the tutor and should be interesting and challenging for the learner (preferably also for the tutor). They offer a chance to collect learner feedback on the course, for example learners can complete a questionnaire on the unit and send it in with their assignment.

> EG This piece of work should be completed in your course booklet. It will be assessed by your tutor and will count towards your grade.
>
> Let your tutor know:
>
> (a) of any difficulty you met within the unit
> (b) your reaction to the course so far.
>
> Please complete the feedback form to give your opinion of this unit.

Sometimes terms other than 'assignment' are used: 'project' – an extended activity sent to a tutor; 'extended exercise' – requiring a number of linked operations, as for example in book-keeping, to enable a tutor to assess learners' ability to combine a number of skills. In all these, the common factor is the involvement of an assessor, usually a professional teacher or trainer.

PLACE	ADVANTAGES	DISADVANTAGES
In text	No separate pieces of paper to get lost	Can be changed only when text is reprinted (unless errata slips are used). Yet may need change for variety, etc.
In separate booklet	Easily updated/issued annually. Convenient: all in one place.	Course writer may not want the learner to see all assignments at once: it may be too daunting. Cannot take into account learner feedback from earlier assignments.
Issued separately	Flexible: can be written at short notice and using learner feedback. Learner gets assignments at a time controlled by tutor/college/writer.	Learner cannot see course as a whole. Someone will have to issue papers. Papers may get lost.

Fig. 2: Positioning of assignments

CL For each question, activity or assignment, ask:

- is it relevant to the unit's stated objective(s)?
- is the purpose clear?
- is the wording/structure clear?
- are the tests varied?
- are the tests manageable?

- if you are involving other people, have you prepared notes for them?

- is each objective tested twice (during and at the end of the unit)?

Have other people commented on your assessment tests? Have you improved the tests in the light of their comments?

4. Feedback

[O] This section helps you provide feedback, so learners can assess the adequacy of their responses to questions, activities and assignments.

[I] From the previous section you'll be aware that assessment questions are important because they keep the learner active. But the questions do not in themselves ensure learning: learners also need feedback on their responses, both as they move through the course (i.e. via the self-completion tests) and at the end (for example, via an activity or an assignment).

Feedback in the text is the written equivalent of face-to-face discussion in a conventional classroom or training session.

This section looks first at what constitutes 'good feedback' generally. It then moves on to feedback for each of: self-completion tests, activities and assignments.

What is good feedback?

Whatever the context – in class or in the text – feedback should always meet certain requirements. Learners need:

- not just the right answer but also to see how it is reached
- information on their own performance, in particular where they may have gone wrong
- a clear picture of what they should do next and in what order
- confidence to move on to the next stage of learning
- confidence in assessing their own performance and thus in becoming more self-directed in their learning.

Feedback on self-completion tests

For self-completion tests full feedback should be included in the text. Thus with these assessment tests you will need to cover, within reason, every possible learner response. With multiple choice questions, for example, you will have to provide comment on every alternative. You will need to give more than just the correct answer but to go on to show how this is arrived at, as in the example below, a true/false self-completion test.

EG Before we look at the other rooms in your home, let's consider some of the things people say about saving energy. Are the following statements True (T) or False (F)?

1. Keeping the immersion heater on all day is cheaper than switching it on only when you need hot water T/F ☐
2. The best place for radiator is under the window T/F ☐
3. Drawing the curtains at dusk saves almost as much heat as double-glazing T/F ☐

ANSWERS

1. False, because you are not taking advantage of cheap tariffs.
2. False, as you will be heating up the coldest air in the room – the air that is coming in from outside. But if you have good double-glazing it is just as cheap to have the radiator under the window as anywhere else in the room.
3. True, because after sunset the outside temperature lowers dramatically. The thick curtains will act as a form of insulation.

If the learner has answered correctly, you need to reinforce and extend this. If, on the other hand, the learner is wrong, it is your responsibility to respond constructively. You might need, for example, to:

- explain why they went wrong
- refer them to the appropriate part of the unit and/or another resource
- suggest they contact their supporter.

Feedback for self-completion tests, unlike that for activities and assignments, is provided in the text itself. You need to decide where to place this. In particular, you need to ask: should the feedback be hidden from the learner and if so, how hidden? If a question is to whet learners' appetite for forthcoming sections, there may be little point in hiding the response. But if it is to test learners' ability to recall five key points already covered, it may be better hidden. Figure 3 might help you decide between the alternatives.

Feedback on activities

It is more difficult to provide standard feedback to cover every possible response to activities. This is because activities are so much more open-ended than self-completion tests. You cannot anticipate exactly what will happen when learners try their learning out 'for real'.

There are two ways of handling this: some general comment in the text and/or feedback from a supporter. If you choose the latter option you should consider giving the supporter guidance on how to give feedback. There are good reasons for using a supporter. Supporters are well-placed to help the learner practise new skills. They can also give encouragement and advice. The example below is from a unit on 'safe cycling'. Together with the learner's unit, these notes would help parents give feedback to their child.

EG *Parents' notes*

The purpose of this test is to make sure that the bearings are checked for correct adjustment. (Although 'he' is used, the test is the same for girls.)

1. Place the bike in an open, flat area and ask him how many bearing checks there are. The correct answer is three. If he gives an incorrect answer remind him of dry test; tightness check; looseness test.
2. Ask him to carry out the three checks.
3. Ensure he turns the bike upside down, and that he makes sure it is steady.

Note: The checks may be carried out in any order.

Position of feedback	*Advantages*	*Disadvantages*	*Notes*
Straight after the question	Continuity	Learners may 'cheat', i.e. read on before they have answered the question	1
At back of unit/ upside down on next page	Hidden	Awkward for learners to find; learners may ignore them	2
On request from a supporter	Hidden; chance to monitor progress; supporter can supplement standard feedback	Possible delay; requires admin. support and forethought	3

Notes

1. You could issue a 'cover card' for learners to cover up the feedback sections of the unit. You could print on the card certain essential course information, for example, definition of important concepts, a key to what symbols mean, a checklist. This makes it more likely that learners will use the card.

2. If you group answers together in order, at the end of a unit, it is possible that learners will see the answer to a forthcoming question. You can avoid this by scrambling the order of answers in the unit (3, 7, 1, 8, etc). Thus when learners read the answer to question 1 they will not easily find the answer to the next question they will be asked.

3. The supporter (who need not be a tutor) would need to be easily available when the learner wants feedback.

Fig. 3: Position of feedback

Feedback on assignments

You should use an assignment when the learner needs feedback from a professional teacher or trainer. Since professional time is expensive, you should use it sparingly. You may, for example, need a tutor to certify that a learner has reached a certain standard, to satisfy an awarding body.

As with activities, you will need to consider producing guidance notes for tutors. They could include, for example, criteria for assessing learners' work; the kinds of comment to make on different levels of learner performance; examples of marked scripts.

Assignments also give the tutor an opportunity to carry out an integrating role – putting the course together by referring back to previous work, looking forward to future assignments, commenting on learner progress. The tutor can comment on learners' views of the course and on any difficulties they may have encountered.

CL Have you anticipated, and provided for, a range of possible responses?

Have you reinforced the good response?

Have you provided help to learners whose response is inadequate?

Have you provided notes for supporters and/or tutors?

Have you used your friend/colleague to comment on the feedback you have written? Have you made any necessary modifications?

5. Writing

[O] This section helps you:

- structure your unit

- link together the parts of your unit you have already produced (i.e. objectives, questions, activities and feedback)

- write new sections (for example introductions and endings)

- develop a straightforward writing style

- monitor and improve your style

- get started!

[I] Your unit should be the written equivalent of the easy, informal approach taken by a good teacher/trainer. The structure of your unit, and your written style, should reassure learners that their needs have been anticipated and met. The words you use are only a part of this process: design, layout and illustration are covered in later sections.

This book recommends an approach to the writing task: objective first, then assessment tests with feedback, and only then the main text. This sequence has been found to work well by many writers of flexible learning materials. You could, or course, choose some other sequence, for example, writing the assessment tests first. What is important is the quality of the end product.

Structuring your unit

If you have followed the advice given in earlier sections of this book you will by now have produced objectives, tests of the objectives (questions, activities and assignments) and feedback on the tests. You now need to put these building blocks into the required order. This will help you see the unit's structure, and plan your linking sections. It will also guarantee a unit that is structured in a way that makes sense to learners.

Figure 4 gives an example of one structure. This is deliberately ambitious to show how many and varied are the means you can use to gain the degree of interaction necessary in a flexible learning unit. You probably won't need as many different elements in your own text. The unit elements are set out on the left-hand side and the purpose of each is given in the right-hand column.

[↻] Plan the structure of your own unit. Get feedback on it.

Introductions, endings and links

You will see from Figure 4 that some new material has to be written. In particular you need a way of opening your unit, a way of closing it and a way of linking the various parts together. Some ideas for each of these are given below.

[CL] *Introductions*
Title
Contents list (or content map)
Unit number (if in a sequence)
List of what the learner should have done previously
List of what the learner needs to have to hand (e.g. any equipment)
Indication of likely time the unit will take

[CL] *Endings*
Summary of main points
Checklist
Ideas for revision
A look forward to a future unit
Optional extra work

[CL] *Signposts*
Route learners through the unit by headings. These should relate to the objectives and emphasise the structure of the unit.
Alert learners to what is to come, e.g. 'I shall set out three approaches. .'
Indicate the beginning and ending, e.g. 'To begin with . . . ', 'To finish, answer this question'.
Emphasise important points, e.g. 'The key point is . . . '

Unit elements	*Purpose of element*
Introduction(s)	Builds learners' confidence, interest and anticipation; helps them to prepare for what is to come
* Orienting questions	Informal questions to focus learners' attention
* Objectives	Help learners see what is expected of them
Text 1	Provides necessary content
* SCT 1	Tests Objective 1
* Feedback on SCT 1	Helps learners assess their response
Text: a case study	Helps learners apply content to a real life example
* Exercise based on the case study	Tests Objective 2
Text	Provides necessary content
* An activity with check-list and supporters' notes	Gives practice on Objectives 1 and 2 combined; helps learners apply unit to own situation
Text	Provides detailed examples necessary for Objective 3
* SCT 2	Based on preceding examples
* Feedback on SCT 2	Allows learners to assess progress
Summary/checklist	Reminds learners of main points
Concluding comment	Looks forward to next unit
* Assignment	Tests Objectives 1 – 3 combined
* Review questions	Offer learners a further chance to check mastery of objectives
Optional extra work	Helps learners who need more practice/work at a higher level

Note: (i) SCT - self-completion test
(ii) *Elements with an asterisk will already have been written. If you have carried out the work suggested earlier you will have already written the most important (and difficult) parts of the unit.

Fig. 4: Structure of a unit

Show relationships within the subject matter, for example, 'However . . .', 'Because. . .', 'So. . .'

Tips on writing style

There are a number of generally agreed principles of good writing. Some of these are summarised below.

Keep it simple
If you have to use a technical word, make sure it's necessary and help the learner use it.

Keep it short
The shorter the word usually the better; avoid words containing many syllables. See Figure 5 for examples.

The shorter the sentence usually the better; aim for 20 words maximum. See Figure 6 for wordy examples and their shorter equivalents.

The shorter the paragraph usually the better; aim for 65 – 91 words, 5 – 7 lines.

The shorter the section within a unit usually the better.

Remember also that you do need some variety in your style.

Use examples
Use examples – concrete details bring points to life.

Write directly
Use the positive rather than the negative. For example, 'It is common' rather than 'It is not uncommon'.

Use the active rather than the passive. For example, 'You considered immigration' rather than 'Immigration was considered'.

Use the personal rather than the impersonal: 'I mentioned . . .' rather than 'It was mentioned . . .'

Use clear signposting. This helps learners see where they are and to feel comfortable. (See the checklist on signposting given earlier.)

Use visuals

Use illustrations wherever possible; see the next section. The example below shows the impact of a simple illustration.

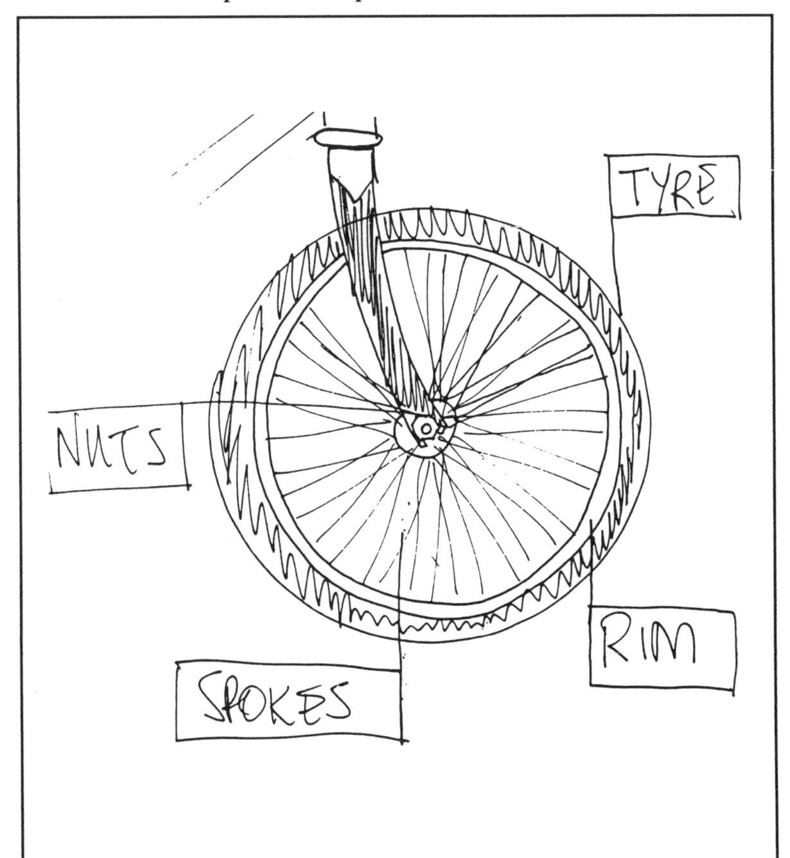

Wheels

The NUTS fix the centre of the wheel to the frame of the bike. The SPOKES connect the centre of the wheel to the RIM. The SPOKES give the wheel strength and keep it straight. The TYRE gives a soft surface for the bike to ride on and helps the wheel to grip the road surface.

Long word	*Short word*
accelerate	speed up
advantageous	useful
anticipate	expect
approximately	about
ascertain	find out
assistance	help
component	part
consequently	so
demonstrate	show
dominant	main
emphasise	stress
endeavour	try
firstly	first
generate	produce
initiate	start
investigate	look into
locate	find
methodology	methods
personnel	people
principal	main
proportion	part
purchase	buy
terminate	end
utilise	use

Fig. 5: Long words and their short equivalents

Wordy English	*Better English*
it is apparent therefore that	so
due to the fact that	because
with the result that	so
is not in a position to	cannot, can't
in connection with	about
in order to	to
in spite of the fact that	although
arrive at a decision	decide
gives positive encouragement to	encourages
bring to a conclusion	finish
if it is assumed that	if
in the vicinity of	near
a proportion of	some
at a later date	later
at that point in time	then

Fig. 6: shortening wordy English

Ask your colleague/friend to check your style, using the advice given in this section.

You might also like to check the style of textbooks and other printed resources used by your learners.

How to improve your style

There are two major points here. First, use to the full the circular process suggested in this book. Second, use readability tests.

The drafting process

This book has stressed the value of drafting and redrafting your work. The process is summarised below.

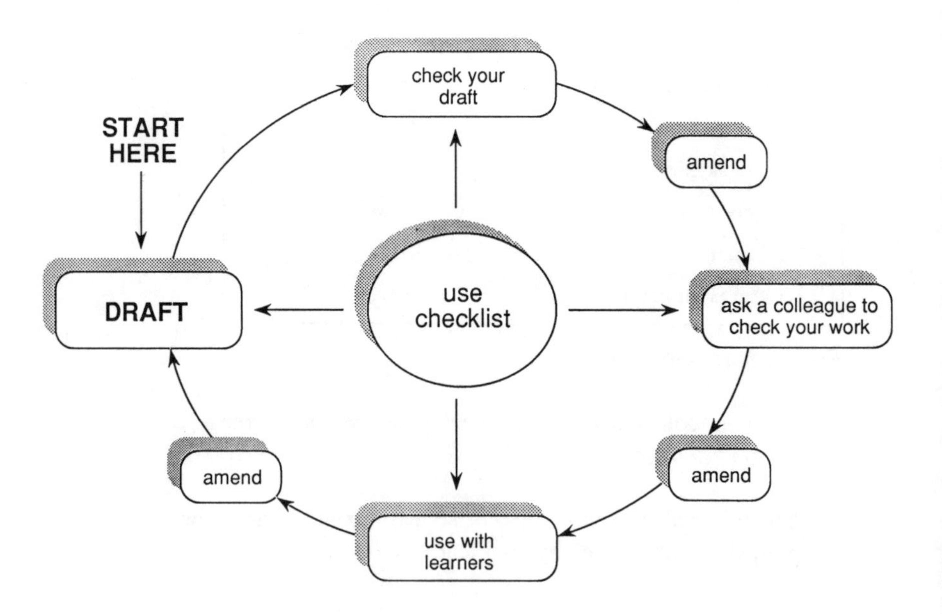

This requires you to submit your work to the scrutiny of other people. You have to welcome criticism because that's the way to improve. You need to go round and round the cycle until you're happy with your work. For more on this, see section 9 on piloting.

Readability tests

Two tests will give you an idea of how readable your prose is: the Cloze Test and the Fog Index. You should also read your work aloud.

The Cloze Test Take a passage of your own text, about 250 words long. Leave a 35-word run-in and then delete the 36th word and every tenth word thereafter (46th, 56th, 66th, 76th, etc.). Stop deleting words when you have deleted 20. An easy way to blank out the words is simply to stick a disguise of Blutack on top. It's better if the reader doesn't know the length of the missing word. But this would mean specially preparing the passage and is probably not worth the trouble in this case.

Now select one (or several) of the people in your target group of learners and try it out. Cloze is particularly useful as part of piloting. If they fail to provide the correct words or a totally acceptable alternative in at least 13 cases out of 20, then the text is too difficult.

If this is the result, then modify the passage by simplifying the language, shortening the sentences and avoiding the use of long or difficult words.

The Modified Fog Index Take a sample passage of about 100 words (several samples would give a better guide but will take more time).

Count all the long words (three syllables or more) in the sample. Then work out the average sentence length of the complete sentences within the sample. You do this by dividing the total number of words by the number of complete sentences.

Then apply the following formula:

$$\text{Reading age (ra)} = \frac{(\text{Average sentence length} + \text{long words}) \times 2}{5} + 5$$

Thus, if the average sentence length was 20 words and there were four long words, then:

$$ra = \frac{(20 \times 4) \times 2}{5} + 5 \qquad ra = \frac{48}{5} + 5 \qquad ra = 9.6 + 5$$

Reading age = 14.6. That is, the passage is suitable for the average reader of 14.6 years.

Generally you should be aiming at around 12. Robert Gunning, who developed the Fog Index (in *The Technique of Effective Writing*, 1952) applied the test to a number of successful authors. He found that they all came out with a score of 11 or below.

A score above 20 indicates that the text is for the highly literate, and may well be hard for anyone.

A simpler measure is just to work out the average number of long words (three syllables or more) in each sentence. If the score is more than three then the writing is likely to be too difficult.

Reading aloud Read your material out aloud or get your colleague to do this while you listen. This will highlight awkward passages that need rewriting.

Apply these tests to your own writing. Apply them, too, to textbooks and other printed materials used by your learners.

How to get started

Get organised

Plan meticulously: the structure of your unit; the detail of your working environment; how you will spend your time.

- Find a block of time you can commit to writing.

- Find a quiet place.

- Have all your materials to hand.

Tackle it bit by bit

- Write the unit in bits; then you have only to stitch the bits together.
- Write first the bits you find easiest.
- If writing on paper, give yourself plenty of space for modification.

Set deadlines

- Set manageable deadlines.
- Produce the first draft quickly.
- Allow enough time. The time you need will depend upon circumstances but assume it will take you around 10 hours to write a decent draft of material that will occupy one hour of learners' time. (In the section on Scheduling I quote up to a further 10 hours for additional work undertaken later in the production cycle.)
- Write the first draft *quickly*, leaving time for changes later.
- Circulate the first draft *early* to get comments on it; allow yourself time to use these comments.

Use colleagues

- to draft with you.
- as a spur – by promising them materials on a set date.
- as a sounding-board.
- to get comments.

[CL] Have you planned the unit's structure?

Have you prepared the beginning?

Have you prepared the ending?

In your writing have you:

- signposted the learner?
- used shorter rather than longer: words, sentences, paragraphs and sections?
- used the Cloze Test and/or the Fog Index and read your work aloud?
- helped the learner *use* any necessary technical terms?
- used examples?
- used the positive, the personal and the active?
- used illustrations?

Have you used your colleague(s)/learners to the full?

Have you amended your style in the light of their comments?

6. Illustrations

O This section helps you use illustrations within your unit.

I Effective visuals help learners in a number of ways:

- by conveying information hard to put into words (for example how a machine works)
- by creating attractive, welcoming learning materials.

Illustrations are particularly important for learners who find pages of dense text off-putting.

Types of illustration

Figure 7 below sets out different kinds of illustration.

Type of Illustration	*Purpose*	*Example*
Photos, drawings	Show what things look like; convey atmosphere	The plug in the Appendix
Drawings, cut-away diagrams	Show how things work	Bicycle wheel in Section 5
Graphs, time lines, bar charts, pie charts blocks, graphs	Show: • size/extent • relation between two or more quantities • change over time	The examples from Report Writing, below
Icons, symbols	Show learning features in the text	The icons used in this book
Cartoons	Lighten/enliven text	Open College/Foster Bros example, overleaf
Flowcharts, algorithms, logical trees	Show structure, sequence	The examples in the Production section of this book

Fig. 7: Uses of illustrations

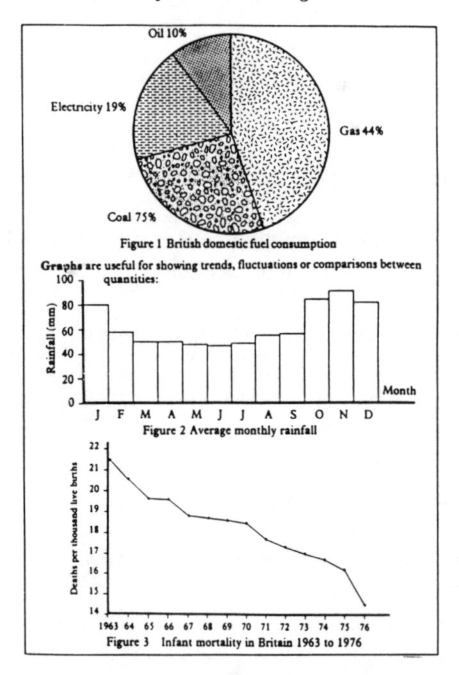

Figure 1 British domestic fuel consumption

Figure 2 Average monthly rainfall

Figure 3 Infant mortality in Britain 1963 to 1976

Ways of showing quantity: extracts from 'Report Writing' by Roger Lewis and John Inglis, pp89, 90,91, published by and reproduced by permission of the National Extension College.

Reproduced by permission of Open College/Foster Brother YTS Programme 1989

Tips on using illustrations

The following tips will help you to use illustrations to maximum effect.

- Illustrations do not need to be complex – in fact, the simpler they are, usually the easier it is to learn from them. You don't have to be a professional artist, just 'good at drawing'. If you are not particularly skilled, you will probably find a friend or colleague who can help.

- With illustrations, as with all other components of your unit, you should get learner reactions to your ideas.

- Some illustrations come ready-made. You can buy whole books full of graphics which you can cut out and use directly in your unit. These are copyright free and are available from good art shops – see the example overleaf.

- It is a good idea to use as wide a range of types of illustration as you can, but don't fall into the trap of using illustrations just for the sake of it: each illustration should serve a purpose.

- You should refer in the text to your illustrations and draw learners' attention to key parts of a drawing or diagram where necessary.

- You should give each illustration a caption.

- When selecting illustrations bear in mind the method you plan to use for producing copies of your unit. Some photographs, for example, will not photocopy well.

Could be used to show when an assignment is due

Could be used to show the learner when to refer to a textbook

Could be used to show when to telephone a tutor

From *How to Communicate with the Learner*, NCET, page 91

CL

Does each illustration have a purpose?
Have you tested your illustrations on learners?
Have you kept your illustrations simple?
Have you referred to your illustrations in the text?
Have you given each illustration a caption?

As before, test your ideas for illustration on your colleague.

7. Design

O This section helps you design and lay out your unit.

I Good design is vital: it helps the learner concentrate on the substance of your unit. It ensures that:

- key learning points stand out visually
- learners find the unit attractive to handle and use.

This section first summarises what 'design' covers. It then lists some of the more important aspects of design, on which you will have to take decisions. It concludes with a discussion of 'house style'.

What is design?

The word 'design' covers all aspects of the appearance of your unit, including the number of words on a page, the use of white space, the size and style of type. A more detailed list is set out in the checklist below.

CL Number of words per page
Size and style of typeface (and how many used)
Number and style of illustrations
Use of colour
Use of space
Use of emphasis
Paper size, orientation and thickness
Appearance of cover
Use of icons/symbols
Placing of answers/feedback
Width of margins/line length of type
Ways of showing headings

portrait landscape

Paper orientation

Key design issues

This book can do little more than suggest the main aspects of design over which you must take decisions. Further advice can be found in the Resources List.

Typesize: the size of letters and other marks on the page, measured in 'points'. The typesize should be neither too large nor too small – 10 or 12 point is usually appropriate, as in the examples below. Note that some typefaces are wider than others for the same point size.

Activities, which encourage learners to apply their learning to the world outside the unit (Times 12 point)

Activities, which encourage learners to apply their learning to the world outside the unit (Times 10 point)

Activities, which encourage learners to apply their learning to the world outside the unit (Helvetica 12 point)

Activities, which encourage learners to apply their learning to the world outside the unit (Helvetica 10 point)

Typeface: the style in which the type is cut. Note the differences between Times and Helvetica above. Times is 'serif'; i.e. some letters, such as i and p have short cross strokes, whereas Helvetica is 'sanserif' (without the cross strokes).

Serif - Times	*Sanserif - Helvetica*
H	H
I	I
f	f

Serifs are generally reckoned to improve text legibility.

Line length or the width from margin to margin. The rule of moderation applies here too. Lines should be neither too long nor too short. With lines that are too long the eye gets lost between the end of one line and the start of the next; lines that are too short unsettle readers. Long lines of small print cause particular problems.

Space between words. Too little and the words seem to join together; too much and reading flow is interrupted.

Showing a new paragraph. New paragraphs are usually shown nowadays by leaving a line space and continuing the new paragraph hard against the left-hand margin. Alternatively, paragraphs can be shown by 'indenting' the first word of the line, i.e. beginning several letter spaces from the left-hand margin.

Use of emphasis. You will sometimes need to emphasise a word or phrase, for example to highlight a key term. Emphasis can be shown by using bold, italics, capitals, or by underlining. The first – bold – is most common now. You should emphasise only occasionally, otherwise the effect is lost, and the text looks fussy.

Lists. Generally use asterisks or 'bullets' to show items in a list. Use numbers (1, 2, 3, 4, etc.) only when you go on to refer to each point by its number; for example "for all the cases covered by (1) above . . . On the other hand, examples of (2) . . ."

Headings. I mentioned these in the section on Writing. You should keep headings simple, with few levels (for example main headings and one level of sub-heading). Headings should relate closely to the objectives of the unit. Keeping your unit to one hour of learning time should make this easy.

You can show headings in a number of ways: by a different 'point' size, by using bold or italics, by capitals or by the use of space (the more space around a heading the greater its importance). Code your headings as you draft: main headings as A, sub-headings as B etc. Later you can translate these into your chosen design features.

Use of space. This is very important. You will develop an eye for clear, well laid-out and attractive pages. The eye is more use than any set of design rules.

Conclusion
You will need to consider the effect of a number of the above points, in combination.

See Figure 8 for an example, which shows the effect of changing type-size, line length and spacing.

Figure 12.2: Varying Line Widths and Spacing

Key: The long lines in A are more difficult to read than the shorter ones in B. However, extra space between the longer lines, as in C and D, may somewhat improve on A's legibility. With a larger type-size (E), the spacing and line width of D is even more legible.

A Using more columns, with a smaller type-size, enables you to get more words on a page. The consequent saving in paper, however, is offset by the fact that readers may be put off by pages that are too heavy with print. Apart from being more difficult to read, densely-printed

B Using more columns, with a smaller type-size, enables you to get more words on a page. The consequent saving in paper, however, is offset by the fact that readers may be put off by pages that are too heavy with print. Apart from

C Using more columns, with a smaller type-size, enables you to get more words on a page. The consequent saving in paper, however, is offset by the fact that readers may be put off by pages that are too heavy with print. Apart from being more difficult to read, densely-printed

D Using more columns, with a smaller type-size, enables you to get more words on a page. The consequent saving in paper, however, is offset by the fact that readers may be put off by pages that are too heavy with print. Apart from being more difficult to read, densely-printed

E Using more columns, with a smaller type-size, enables you to get more words on a page. The consequent saving in paper, however, is offset by the fact that readers may be put off by pages that are too heavy with print. Apart from

Fig. 8: Varying line widths and spacing
Reproduced with acknowledgement from *Teaching Through Self-Instruction*, Derek Rowntree, Kogan Page, 1986 (p.285).

The example below shows different ways of using layout.

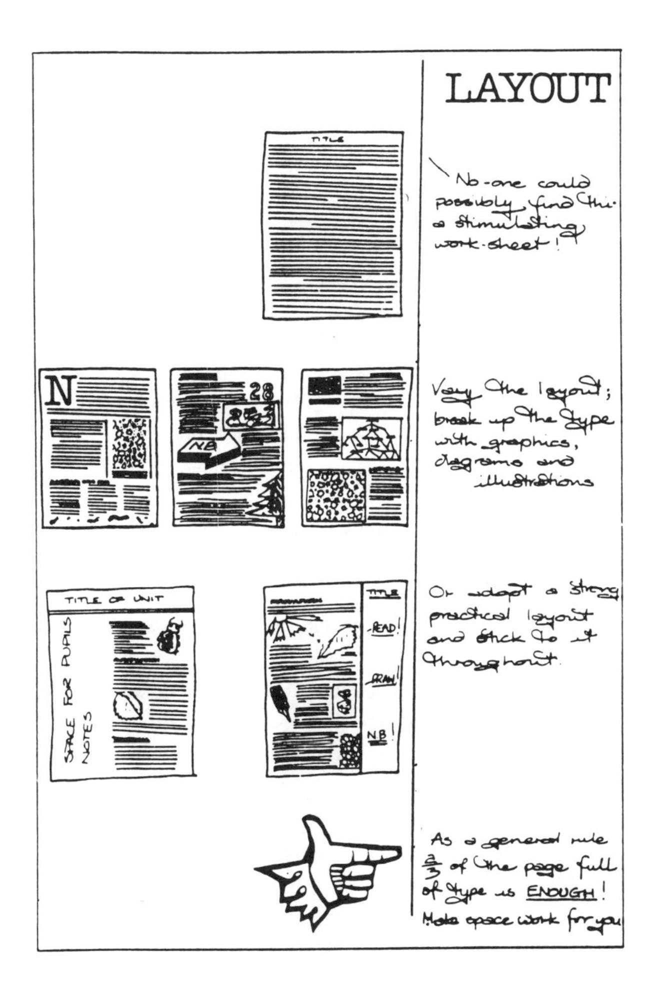

From *How to communicate with the Learner*, NCET, p.90

House style

Consistency is vital. House rules help you and others who may be involved such as a typist, to achieve this. You need to draw up your own set of rules, covering points such as those made earlier in this section: how different levels of heading will be set out, how emphases will be conveyed, how paragraphs will be started. An example, which you should feel free to add to or adapt, is given below. (Earlier sections will suggest possible extra material.)

House Style

Number all pages

New para: leave one clear line space

Headings level A - all caps.; new line
B - first letter of each word cap.; new line
C - embolden and run on

Illustrations: keep these (figures, table etc.) on separate sheets and with captions (for pasting in later)

Footnotes: none (if necessary, include at end of unit as notes)

Quotations: single inverted commas except where double inverted commas are needed to show a quotation within a quotation; for quotes of 5 lines or more leave a line of space above and below.

Spelling: in general follow *Oxford English Dictionary*, e.g. judgement, inquire, focused, biased, cooperate

Abbreviations: no full stop - 13cm; Dr; Ltd; BBC

Dates: as 1 May 1989; 1980s; twentieth century

Number: below 10 write in full; above 10, in figures (e.g., eight, 780)

For highlighting text within a para: use bold

CL

Have you followed the 'not too' advice?

- typesize: neither too large nor too small
- typeface; not too fussy
- line length; neither too long nor too short
- space between words; neither too much not too little
- emphasis; not too frequent
- headings; not too many
- space; neither too much nor too little on each page.

Have you drafted a set of house rules?

Have you asked your colleague to comment on your ideas for design?

Have you modified your plans in the light of your colleague's comments?

8. Production

O This section helps you take your unit through from first draft to final text, ready for distribution and use.

I The final appearance of your unit is important. It will determine how easy your learners find to use it. A number of other people will also make judgements on your work – teachers or trainers, parents, colleagues etc. Their judgements will often be based on a fairly superficial response to the look of your unit.

There are other reasons why you should spend time on the final stages of your unit's production. In conventional publishing a number of people usually carry out these stages: different people are often used to edit, design, illustrate, proof-read, pilot, print and bind the material. This long chain is often badly managed with the following unfortunate results:

- the writer's intentions are frustrated; changes are often made in ignorance
- costs escalate
- the production process is very slow, subject to delay at every stage.

If you – the writer – stay in charge of the full production process you will avoid these dangers.

So, for a number of reasons – some strictly educational, others practical and yet others promotional – you need to attend to the final stage of production. Your work, sadly, is not over once the content and learning methods have been decided!

Production Stages

The main stages of production are set out below. The notes give more information on each stage.

Stage	*Note*
First full draft	1
First review	2, 3, 4
Printing	5
Pilot	6
Second review	7
Copy and bind	8, 9
Distribute	10

Notes

1. First full draft

This is the first full draft of the unit, incorporating your work at all the earlier stages. If you have been drafting directly on the computer, you will need to get material into the correct sequence (see Writing, Fig. 4) and edit it in accordance with the house rules you have decided to follow (see Design).

If you have been drafting on paper you will need to word process the materials, again following your house rules. Make sure you leave room for illustrations; you can paste these in after word processing is completed.

2. First review

This includes your own review of the unit, using the checklists provide earlier, and your colleague's. Seeing the full text, in its correct order, always shows new things to change.

3. Editing
Your review is effectively a form of 'editing'. Editing is a scrutiny of the unit from a number of points of view, including:

- content; accuracy, interpretation, coverage
- learning effectiveness; how easy it is to learn from the unit
- clarity and style of language; grammar, spelling, punctuation, paragraphing
- conformity to house rules; captions, headings, details on title page.

In publishing, these different types of editing are referred to variously, for example subject editing (content); open learning editing (learning effectiveness); copy editing (English and house rules); proof-reading (final check on detailed changes).

4. Ready for piloting
The end result of your review is to decide what changes you feel necessary before the material is piloted with learners and to make those changes. Try to get it as near perfect as you can: errors, and especially small ones like misprints, distract learners and create a bad impression, leading to unnecessarily harsh feedback.

5. Printing
If you do your own printing from a word processor, use a daisy-wheel printer, or better still, a laser printer. Avoid dot-matrix printers if you can.

6. Pilot
This is so important that the whole of the next section is devoted to it. Whatever else you cut, you shouldn't cut the piloting stage.

7. Second review
At this stage you review the results of the pilot and decide on and make the changes you judge necessary. See note 3 on editing: this is your final chance to check all aspects of your unit. You should check particularly that any post-piloting changes are accurate and correct.

8. Copying

The method of reproducing your unit will depend on the number of copies you need and the facilities at your disposal; photocopying is usually the easiest and most economical way.

9. Binding

After copying, sheets – including the cover – have to be placed in the correct order ('collated') and fixed together.

For a small number of sheets, stapling is best. Other alternatives are insertion in a ring binder, wire binding, cone binding, or a plastic spine. Some of these are illustrated below.

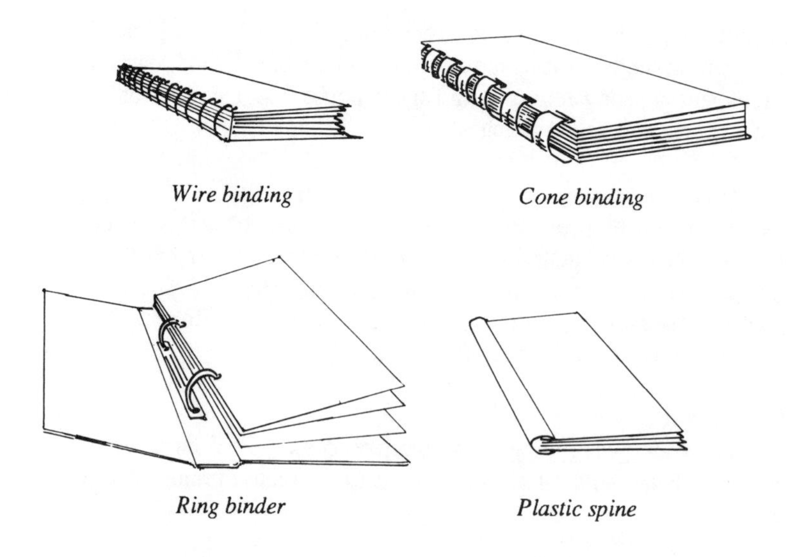

Wire binding *Cone binding*

Ring binder *Plastic spine*

Think through all the implications before choosing your method. For example:

- you need access to special equipment for cone/wire binding
- plastic spines have a habit of sliding off
- for ring binding you incur the expense of a binder and you have to punch holes accurately in the sheets.

10. Distribution
Copies may be passed on by hand to learners, held for their collection in a resource centre, or sent through the post.

Scheduling

The above sequence may sound complex. In fact it is logical and straightforward but it does require you to be organised. Much learning material production becomes lengthy and stressful because there is slippage at every stage. Setting out realistic deadlines, and keeping to them is the key to success. Scheduling is covered later (Section 11).

Audio tape production

In this book I assume that print is your main medium. But audio cassette can also be useful and relatively easy to produce. You might choose, for example, to use audio cassette for discussion or a case study, to talk learners through a complex activity, or for practising a foreign language. The production sequence, summarised below, is similar to that for print.

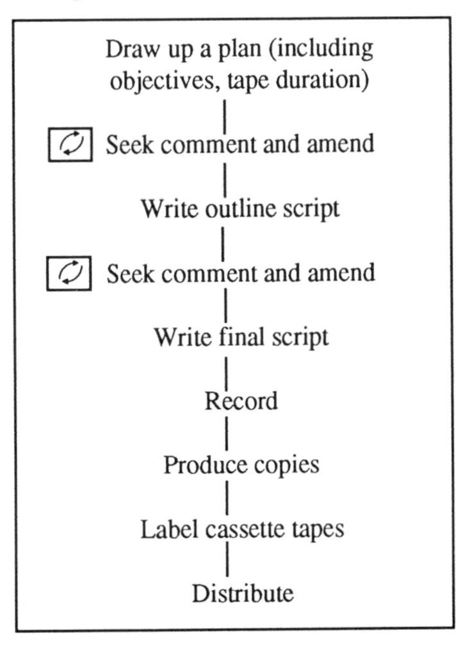

I have kept the sequence as simple as possible. In particular, I assume that you are recording in one session, without tape editing, in a suitable room (not necessarily a purpose-built studio). More ambitious tapes would require location recording and/or editing. If you need further advice see the Resources list.

You should be able to find a local school or college with tape copying facilities. Audio-tape is an inexpensive medium; you should be able to produce even small runs for less than one pound per tape (1990 prices).

You will need to clear any material in copyright, including music. See Section 12.

CL Check that you have planned for/carried out the following:

- a first full draft
- your, and a colleague's, review
- changes after the review
- a pilot
- changes after the pilot
- production method
- collating and binding
- distribution

(or the audio equivalents).

9. Pilot

[O] This section helps you try out your unit with learners.

[I] The most valuable feedback comes from your target users – after all, that's who you're producing the unit for. If it doesn't work for them you've failed – however happy your colleagues may be with what you have written. In this section I define piloting and help you plan your pilot.

What is piloting?

Piloting is the trial of your unit, with learners in the target population. It gives you the chance to see how the unit works, to identify problems and to ask for comments on particular features. Learners work though the unit, answering the questions and carrying out the activities. Piloting is small-scale and informal. Its overriding purpose it to help you improve the unit.

How to run a pilot

The activities involved in piloting are set out below, together with notes.

Stage	*Note*
choose learners	1
brief learners	2
carry out the pilot	3
analyse feedback; make changes	4

Notes

1. You need up to six representative learners from the target group. They obviously have to be willing and available when you want them. You could reward them in some way, for example by a snack meal and mention in the acknowledgements of the final product.

2. If possible, get the learners together. (If this is not possible, see the note on piloting at a distance). Explain the purpose – that it's the unit that's being tested, not them; you want to know what they think (stress this, because learners usually err on the side of 'politeness'). Give examples of the kinds of feedback you want and when and how you want them made (see 3 below).

   It may be better for a colleague to carry out the briefing and pilot stages, if you feel learners would be more honest and relaxed without you present as the unit author.

3. This is where you collect data on the unit's effectiveness. See the checklist on p.55 for things to look for. There are a number of ways by which you can collect the data, as shown below.

   - Get learners to complete a pre-test to show their state of knowledge or skill before starting the unit; then get them to complete a post-test after they have worked through the unit. This establishes what the unit has taught them.

     Watch learners as they work through their unit. Complete a record sheet such as that on page 56 to log your observations, the learners' comments and your ideas for changes to the unit. (One copy of the form is filled in as an example and one is blank for you to copy should you wish.)

   - Try not to intervene as learners work on the unit. But if you do have to, think about putting this extra help into the next draft of the unit.

   - Ask learners to write on the pages of the unit and complete the assessment tests within it; collect these and analyse them later.

   - Discuss the unit with the learners when they have finished working though it, by following a checklist of key questions.

   - Thank learners at the end of the pilot and explain what you will do with their comments and work.

4. Even with a small number of learners you should have gained some useful feedback from the pilot. This could be in a variety of forms, for example completed units, answers to questions and activities, completed questionnaires and observation sheets, notes from discussion. All this will need analysing. You will then need to decide what to do in the light of the data. Again, a colleague can be helpful here, to bounce ideas off and insist you avoid easy options!

Piloting at a distance

Sometimes you will not be able to get learners together. You can, though, still carry out a pilot using post and telephone. The principles and processes are identical, but you will need to adapt the methods.

If you are piloting at a distance you should:

- focus sharply on the key points
- brief learners by telephone
- send the unit and a questionnaire
- get back the unit and questionnaire
- 'phone learners to get further comment if necessary.

The checklist below gives you some ideas of what to look for in your pilot.

CL Have you made plans to carry out your pilot?

- Where do learners get stuck?
- Are time estimates realistic?
- What do they learn?
- Do they like using the unit?
- Do they learn from, and like, the flexible learning features of your material? Consider:

the objectives
tests and answers
feedback
your style
unit design

} see the earlier checklists on each of these

Record Sheet

Name: TONY STEVENS Date: 11/6/90

Title: WRITING A REPORT Version: 2

Details of learner: 16 – Preparing for Workplace assessment

Starting time: 11.15 Finishing time: 12.40

Unit section no.	Observation of tester	Comments from learner	Proposed action
1	Learner took less time than allowed. ✓	"It looks interesting. I can see what I've got to do."	Change time allocation?
2	Paused at top of p.4 – seemed confused by cross-reference. ✓	—	Improve cross-reference
3	— X	"I don't understand the question."	Rephrase SAQ2 – wording unclear.
4	Confused when he went to library shelves.	—	Activity too open-ended. Restructure, to give more help.
5	Looked back to previous section. ✓	—	Rewrite – better lead-in to this learning point.

Points for discussion at end of session:
Timing – section 1
Cross-reference – section 2
Activity: what further help would he have liked? (4)
Why did he need to refer back? (5)

Notes on record sheet

1. Column 2: √ = correct response to question; X = wrong response to question.
2. Column 4 is filled in at the end of the session, after discussion with the learner.

Record Sheet

Name: .... Date: ....

Title: .... Version: ....

Details of learner:.......................................

Starting time:... Finishing time: ......

Unit section no.	Observation of tester	Comments from learner	Proposed action
1			
2			
3			
4			
5			

Points for discussion at end of session

10. Operation

O — This section helps you maintain your unit effectively once it is in use.

I — As a professional you will have a commitment to quality. This commitment will not cease with the production and distribution of the final copy. However good, the unit will be capable of improvement. With the best will in the world, errors will have crept in and facts will need up-dating. You will also think of ever better ways of presenting your materials, learning from comments your users make.

You need to decide:

- what data you will collect
- how you will collect it
- how you will store it
- when you will act upon it.

Collecting data

Figure 9 overleaf shows some major types of data, their sources and possible methods of collection.

Type of Data	*Source of Data/ Method of Collection*	*Notes*
Learner performance	Scores on pre- and post-tests; assignment results; annotated copies of units/ answers to tests.	
Misprints, errors	Annotated copies of unit Learner comments Teacher comments	See Figure 10 for what to look for
Learner perceptions of unit (ease, attractiveness, relevance etc.)	These may be collected by a number of means: • questionnaires (closed or open or semi-structured) • interviews (telephone or face-to-face; individual and/ or group) • continuing to watch learners use the materials (see Section 9, Pilot) • unsolicited (e.g. letters, telephone calls)	See example below Questionnaires may be enclosed with the unit and returned Various sources may be used in combination e.g. interviews to follow up returned questionnaires Use a standard pad to record unsolicited comments
Perceptions of others (of ease, attractiveness, relevance, etc.)	Sources and methods of collection as for learners (see above box)	'Others': supporters (tutors, teachers, lecturers); subject specialists; sponsors. Get people together for a social event?

Fig. 9: Types and sources of feedback data

EG *Extracts from a feedback questionnaire*

1. How many hours did you spend working on the booklet?

Less than 7 hours ☐ 7-12 hours ☐ 13-18 hours ☐ More than 19 hours ☐

3. Was the amount of information in the course?

Too much ☐ About right ☐ Insufficient ☐

4. How useful has the booklet been to you?

Very useful ☐ Fairly useful ☐ Not useful at all ☐ Don't know yet ☐

8. Please note down two things about the booklet which you particularly liked.

i)
ii)

9. Please note down two things about the booklet which you feel could be improved.

i)
ii)

Storing data

It follows that you might need to store data such as the following:

- learner performance data
- annotated units
- questionnaires
- results of interviews, (transcripts, summaries)
- letters, telephone calls
- tear-off carbonised response/query sheets
- periodic summaries of all the above.

Action

You need to decide:

- when to analyse the feedback (e.g. three months? annually?)
- how/when to decide what action to take.

Action could, for example, take the form of:

1 errata sheets
2 minor changes
3 a new edition, incorporating major changes
4 a complete re-write.

The action you take will depend on the nature of the feedback. For example: for small points such as wrong page numbering, wrong dates (1) above; for fundamental problems with learning design such as people taking three times the time you allocated, learner performance data which consistently shows an objective is not achieved, alternatives (3) or (4) above.

CL

What data will you collect?
What are the best sources of this data?
What methods will you use to collect it?
How will you store it?
When will you analyse it?
When will you act on it?

Errors	*Language*	*Learning Design*	*Out of date*
missing pages	spelling mistakes	unclear objectives	figures
blank pages	punctuation errors	unsuccessful tests	case studies
pages wrongly numbered; pages poorly reproduced		poor feedback (see also check-lists in earlier sections)	new events, acts of parliament etc.
wrong captions			
incomplete or wrong cross-references			

Fig. 10: What to look for

11. Scheduling

[O] This section helps you draw up an action plan for the production of your unit.

Activity	*Likely duration*	*Your own start/ finish dates*	*Your notes*
Plan: decide who will use your material, under what circumstances, what content it will cover, what media you will use	Variable - from one day to three months		
Write objectives	one week		
Write tests, with feedback	one week one week		
Write linking text, introductions etc.	one week		
Decide design, use of illustrations, house rules, etc.	one week		
First draft in agreed layout; yours and a colleague's review	two weeks		
Pilot, review results, make changes	two weeks		
Copy, bind and distribute	one week		
Monitor the unit in use	ongoing		

Notes

1. I assume you are working on a unit that will take the learner one hour to complete. It should, in total, take you 10 – 20 hours of work, at all stages, to product this.

2. For each activity, time is allowed for consultation with colleagues etc. and for the redrafting that usually follows.

3. The 'Duration' column sets out the length of time an activity should take once you are ready to start it.

4. The whole process should take you two to three months (note that I assume in this book that you have already carried out the first activity listed, i.e. planning).

5. Use the third column to set up your own planned dates/ duration and the fourth column for any notes.

12. Copyright

There are two issues here. First, who owns the copyright of what you produce? Second, how do you clear copyright for material from elsewhere that you want to use in your unit?

Who owns the copyright of your unit?

The answer is "it all depends". If you produce the unit in your 'own' time (for example evenings after work) then you will hold the copyright. But if you write it in work time the copyright will rest with your employer. If you are writing as part of the funded project, (for example your unit is produced with Training Agency funding), the funder will hold copyright. You should clarify the position before you start to write.

How do you clear copyright of material you want to use?

If you want to use material that has already appeared elsewhere you will usually have to clear copyright, even if your unit itself will not be sold. To do this you have to write to the copyright holder (who may be an author or publisher) setting out:

- exactly what you wish to use (for example, title of book, date, page, first word/last word)
- the purpose for which you wish to use it (for example GCSE unit for use only within one named school; in-house training programme in a company).

Clearance is usually forthcoming, but it can take some time.

Publishers will often allow material to be used non-commercially – in education and training, without charge. But sometimes you will be asked to pay a fee (for example if you wish to quote from a popular song). Given the twin dangers of delay and possible expense, you may think it wiser to avoid the need to clear copyright in the first place.

See the Resources List for more advice on copyright.

13. Glossary

Several entries in this Glossary draw on *The A-Z of Open Learning*, published by NEC. Readers are referred to this publication for more detail, and for definitions of other words used in open and flexible learning.

Activity: A task within the unit to help learners apply their learning. Activities concentrate on the transfer of competence to the outside world and will frequently involve people not in a direct teaching relationship with learners (colleagues, family and friends).

Assessment: The measurement of learner performance. This may be:

- formal or informal
- exact or rough and ready
- carried out by learners themselves (self-assessment), by other people or by computer
- immediate (as, for example, when the learner is observed carrying out a practical activity) or delayed
- carried out during a course or at its end or both
- closed (as for example, with multiple choice questions) or open (as, for example, with projects).

Assignment: An opportunity for learners to carry out a piece of work for submission to a tutor for feedback and/or grading. Distinguished from self-assessment, where learners themselves are responsible for assessing their own performance, using standard guidance given in the package (see 'project').

Case study: A realistic scenario, either from real life or constructed. Case studies allow learners to explore issues and apply their learning. They may be short or long, simple or elaborate, assessed or non-assessed.

Checklist: A list of questions to help learners review progress and/ or apply their learning and/or complete an activity.

Chunk: A manageable amount of learning, within a unit, for example the amount a learner in the target group might be expected to complete in one study session. The size of a 'chunk' will vary according to the learner, the context and the nature of the material.

Cloze procedure: A method of assessing the readability of text involving the deletion of words (usually every 10th word).

Collate: To place the sheets of a unit in order, before attaching them.

Course: Term used to denote a coherent learning experience, probably containing several units (for example a GCSE course).

Design: All aspects of the physical appearance of a unit.

Distractor: Incorrect option in a multiple choice question.

Editing: The process of checking and preparing a 'unit' for production; covers four main activities: checking the content, the learning effectiveness, the language and conformity to house rules.

When used in the context of audio cassette production 'editing' can be used as above to describe the preparation of a script for recording: the selection of material for content, learning effectiveness and language. It can also be used to describe the process of modifying the recorded material to conform to the agreed script by changing the order of items or deleting sections. This process usually involves cutting and joining the audio tape.

Feedback: The provision of comment: on learners' performance (within the text or via a supporter); on the learning materials themselves (especially from learners).

Flexible learning: Term used to describe the creation or adaptation of learning opportunities to meet the needs of learners and/ or other clients; often used interchangeably with 'open learning' to imply either or both of: delivery more convenient to learners' or clients and/or delivery that consciously seeks to build learners' autonomy giving them opportunities to make choices. If there is a difference between this phrase and 'open learning' it is that 'flexible learning' describes changes to the delivery of courses already in existence.

Fog Index: A formula for assessing the readability of text.

House rules: A set of guidelines used by authors/editors/designers to ensure continuity and consistency in the style and presentation of 'units'. Sometimes also called 'house style'.

Key: The correct answer in a multiple choice question.

Icon: A symbol regularly used within a unit to indicate a function; for example, in this text, an [O] means 'the objective of this section is . . .'

Indenting: Beginning further in from the margin than other lines in the paragraph.

Learner: Term used to describe the user of the unit whether student in a college or university, trainee in a government scheme, employee in a company or pupil in a school.

Matching lists: A self-completion test which presents two lists to learners who have to match items in one list with those in another.

Medium/ media:	The means chosen for transmission of the unit (for example print, audio tape).
Monitoring:	The regular scrutiny of a unit during use to check its effectiveness and acceptability to learners and others.
Multiple choice questions:	A test taking the form of a stem followed by a series of possible answers ('options'). Usually only one of these is correct (the'key') and the others are incorrect (the 'distractors').
Objective:	A statement of what learners should achieve from studying part of a unit; an 'objective' is expressed in terms of the capacities that the learner will acquire and be able to demonstrate. 'Objectives' are sometimes labelled 'pay-offs', 'benefit' or 'outcomes'.
Open learning:	Term used to describe schemes of education and training that consciously provide learners with increased choice over aspects of their learning, such as over what, when, where and how they learn. Open learning is sometimes used to achieve greater convenience of delivery (for example so learners can study away from a fixed place), sometimes (and increasingly) as a strategy to help learners gain greater autonomy.
Option:	One of a series of answers in a multiple choice test.
Orientation (of paper):	The placing and direction of the paper, either portrait or landscape.
Pilot:	The trial of a unit, with learners in the target group prior to the unit's production in finished form. A number of features can be checked in a pilot including style, content, clarity of objectives, level. Data from learners can be gained by various means, including questionnaire and interview. Feedback from piloting is used to improve text.

Point: The basic unit of typographic measurement, which gives the size that a particular typeface will be printed at.

Project: A major piece of work, requiring independent planning and completed over an extended period, usually sent to a tutor for assessment. ('Assignments' tend to be lesser tasks completed in a shorter time.)

Self-completion tests: Questions in the unit to facilitate learning, especially to enable learners to check their grasp of unit content. The tests are usually followed by answers, together with additional comments; this feedback gives learners the information on which to check the adequacy of their response.

Self-completion tests are also called 'self-assessment questions' (SAQs), 'self checks' etc.

(Compare 'activity' which requires the application of concepts or skills to the world *outside* the package.)

Serif: Typeface using short strokes at the ends of arms and stem of letters ('sanserif' – any typeface without serifs).

Signposting: Means used within a unit to help learners establish where they are, where they've come from and where they are going – including introductions and conclusions, linking sentences, icons, cross-references.

Stem: Opening statement in a multiple choice question, followed by a number of possible answers ('options').

Supporter: A person who helps learners use the unit, whether professional (a 'tutor') or non-professional, for example a friend, member of family, colleague.

Tests: Means of gaining data on learner performance, to check the extent to which learners have achieved unit objectives. The tests may be self administered ('self-completion tests') or involve others, whether professionals ('assignments') or non-professionals ('activities'). Tests may be administered before the unit, during it, or at its end. They may take many different forms (see Section 3 on Assessment).

Target group: Learners for whom a unit is intended.

True/false questions: A question in the form of a statement. Learners have to decide whether the statement is true or false.

Tutor: A professional involved in helping learners, for example a lecturer in a university of college, a trainer in industry or a teacher in a school. Tutoring is differentiated from more general support because some degree of subject-matter expertise and teaching or training expertise is usually required. Tutoring may be provided face-to-face, by telephone, through the post or by a combination of these.

Typeface: Style in which letters (and other marks) appear on the page, for example, Courier, Times, Helvetica, Palatino.

Typesize: Size of letters (and other marks) on the page, measured in terms of 'points', for example, 10 pt, 12 pt.

Unit: A coherent piece of learning material, occupying approximately one hour of learner time.

14. Resources List

General

Three useful general resources are:

The Open Learning Pocket Workbook, NCET 1988
For a simple overview.
The A-Z of Open Learning, NEC 1990
For an up-to-date glossary.
Teaching Through Self-Instruction, Kogan Page 1986
For a more detailed approach, particularly relevant to major materials' production projects.

Planning

The Open Learning Pocket Workbook, NCET 1988
An introductory text for help on all aspects of planning open and flexible learning.
The NEC Guide to Open Learning, NEC 1986
A simple, introductory resource on planning the learning material aspect of a scheme.
How to Develop and Manage an Open Learning System, NCET 1985
Gives more detailed advice on planning.
Teaching Through Self-Instruction, Kogan Page 1986
A full treatment of all aspects of planning, with plenty of examples.
How to Find and Adapt Materials and Select Media, NCET 1986
For more on finding and adapting existing learning material, for use in open and flexible learning; and selecting appropriate media.
The Role of Technology in Distance Education, Croom Helm/ St Martin's Press 1984
Has a useful, detailed selection of articles on the use of different media in open learning.
Computer Assisted Training, CITB Management Training Series XA618
A refreshingly practical introduction to the topic.
How to Communicate with the Learner, NCET 1985
Has a section on how to construct packages.

The Schools' Guide to Open Learning, NEC 1986
Of help if you work in a school context. The book is designed both for individual and for workshop use.
Supported Self Study: an Introduction for Teachers, NCET 1988
Will help you set up a trial scheme.
The Open Learning Handbook, Kogan Page 1989
Will help you if you work in higher education and are concerned with cognitive learning.
Developing Courses for Students, McGraw Hill 1981
An authoritative and accessible text on educational technology.

Writing Objectives

How to Help Learners Assess their Progress: Writing Objectives, Self-Assessment Questions and Activities, NCET 1984
Expands the advice given in this book, and refers to a number of extra resources on writing objectives.
Preparing Instructional Objectives, Fearon 1982
A standard work by R J Mager.
Stating Behavioural Objectives for Classroom Instruction, Mac-Millan 1970
Another standard work, by N E Gronlund.
A Guide to the Writing of Objectives, RAF School of Education (no date).
The Armed Forces really understand how to write objectives. Unfortunately this – and similar books from the Army and Navy – are not easily available.
A Workshop on the Writing of Learning Objectives, Coombe Lodge Working Paper 1331, Further Education Staff College 1979
Somewhat dated, but the advice (in this case from T J Russell) is just as relevant today.

Assessment and Feedback

How to Help Learners Assess their Progress: Writing Objectives, Self-Assessment Questions and Activities, NCET 1984
Gives further advice and examples. It has a useful section on writing multiple choice questions.

The Manual of Objective Testing, City and Guilds of London Institute 1977
CGLI is an excellent source of advice on writing 'closed' assessment questions.
How to Write Self-Assessment Questions, Scottish Council for Educational Technology, Open Learning Paper number 302 1983
A very accessible guide to the topic, free at the time of writing (for SCET's address, see later in the Resources List).
Assessing Students. How shall we know them? Harper & Row 1977
A general source on assessment.
Teaching through Self-Instruction, Kogan Page 1986
Chapter 3 is on assessing your learners.
How to Tutor and Support Learners, NCET 1984
Contains details on writing assignments to be marked by a tutor, including the provision of tutor notes.
Tutors' Handbook, Open College 1988
Detailed advice on tutoring in open learning.

Writing

How to Communicate with the Learner, NCET 1985
Covers: characteristics of open learning material; how to construct flexible packages – different starting points, routes and learning styles; how to design a package (including chunking, beginnings, endings, in-text signposting); how to write readable prose; how to get started.
Teaching through Self-Instruction, Kogan Page 1986
Chapter 10 is on making your lesson readable.
Writing for Open Learning, EDU, Staffordshire Polytechnic 1989
Very useful short guide available from PR Kay, Staffordshire Polytechnic, College Road, Stoke on Trent, ST4 2DE.

Illustrations and Design

How to Communicate with the Learner, NCET 1985
For more information on illustrations (kinds, purposes), format and layout.
Teaching through Self-Instruction, Kogan Page 1986
Chapter 9 is on teaching with pictures and chapter 12 on the physical format of your lesson.

Editing for Everyone, NEC 1983
A course on copy-editing, very useful for writers who also want to develop formal editing skills.
Design for Desktop Publishing, Gordon Fraser 1987
This book, by John Miles, is a useful resource for desktop publishing.

Production and Pilot

How to Manage the Production Process, NCET 1986
A detailed guide to the production of open learning materials, from planning through to final product (and including piloting). It also has sections on non-print media. The appendices and booklist are particularly useful. The book tends to assume a team approach rather than a single author/producer carrying out all stages.
Audio Techniques, Vol.9 of the Training Technology Programme, Parthenon Press 1987
A detailed manual of advice on making audio tapes, written by Peter Darnton.

Operation and Scheduling

How to Develop and Manage an Open Learning System, NEC 1989
The second part is on how to manage a scheme, including monitoring. There is a useful appendix on evaluation.
How to Manage the Production Process, NCET 1986
Has a section on what should happen beyond the production of the unit.
Teaching through Self-Instruction, Kogan Page 1986
Chapter 14 covers the construction of questionnaires.

Copyright

NCET has a free Information Sheet on copyright. Write to the NCET address given later in this section.
Copyright Clearance: a practical guide, NCET 1990
A comprehensive guide for those in education.
Teaching through Self-Instruction, Kogan Page 1986
Chapter 15 contains useful advice on copyright.

Glossary

The A-Z of Open Learning, NEC 1990
This is invaluable if you require a full glossary of open and flexible learning terms.

Other Useful Resources

NEC (1985) has published three resources to help learners work together. These are: *Team Working* – a guide to management development groups (for corporate users); *Studying together* (for educational users); *Learning together* (for informal learning groups).
Managing the Learning Process, McGraw Hill 1983
This is a sound and thorough treatment of managing situations to ensure learning in school.
The Department of Employment Training Agency has published useful resources on flexible learning, including material on quality and case studies. Write to the address below for information on what is currently available.

Addresses

The Further Education Unit
Grove House, 2 Orange Street, London WC2H 7WE.
Tel: 071 321 0433

The National Council for Educational Technology (NCET)
3 Devonshire Street, London W1N 2BA. Tel: 071 636 4186
and
Sir William Lyons Road, Science Park, University of Warwick, Coventry CV4 7EZ. Tel: 0203 416994

The National Extension College (NEC)
18 Brooklands Avenue, Cambridge CB2 2HN. Tel: 0223 316644

Open College (OC)
Third Floor, St James's Buildings, Oxford Street, Manchester, M1 6FQ. Tel: 061 228 6415

Scottish Council for Educational Technology (SCET)
Dowanhill, 74 Victoria Crescent Road, Glasgow, G12 9JN.
Tel: 041 334 9314/357/0340
The Learning Systems Unit (LSU) of this organisation has pioneered developments in open and flexible learning.

The Department of Employment Training Agency (TA)
Moorfoot, Sheffield S1 4FQ. Tel: 0742 753275

Appendix: Types of self-completion test

This appendix describes and illustrates the main types of self-completion test:

- multiple choice question
- true/false
- matching list
- sequencing
- completing blanks
- visual
- numerical

Multiple choice question

This is a versatile type of question, well worth your while developing. It contains a statement (stem) followed by a series of possible answers (options). One option is correct (the key) and the others (the distractors) are wrong.

EG According to the text, which of the following best distinguishes poetry from prose?

(a) line length
(b) rhyme
(c) imagery
(d) symbolism

True/false

This question asks the learner to indicate which of a list of statements is true and which false.

EG Which of the following are true or untrue statements?

	True	False
(a) If the wheel wobbles when spinning it must be adjusted		
(b) The cycle is unsafe to ride with four spokes loose		
(c) All spoke faults are repaired at the cycle shop		

Matching list

Learners are presented with two lists of data and they have to match items in one list with items from the other.

EG Place in the box following each statement (1-3) the letter corresponding to the heat transfer process involved (A-D).

1. The handle of poker placed on a fire becomes hot
2. Bread can be toasted in front of a fire
3. A fire warms a room

A Radiation
B Radiation and convection
C Radiation, convection and conduction
D Conduction

Sequencing

This provides a list of points and asks the learner to put them in order according to a stated criterion, for example importance, size or sequence.

EG If you were to reduce the lever travel the following five steps would have to be take. Can you please arrange them in the correct order by writing 1, 2, 3, 4 or 5 in each of the boxes.

(a) Tighten locknut ☐
(b) Unscrew adjusting screw ☐
(c) Slacken locknut ☐
(d) Check lever movement ☐
(e) Spin wheel to check no binding ☐

Completing blanks

These questions ask learners to fill blank spaces by selecting appropriate words, phrases or numbers.

EG Complete the following sentences by filling in the blanks, choosing the missing words from the list below.

When devising self-completion questions,

(a) [ ] type questions are most suitable for linking facts and dates, while
(b) [ ] type questions are more appropriate for assembling equipment.

- multiple choice
- matching lists
- sequencing
- completing blanks

Open questions

All the above examples can be called 'closed' questions; the learner is given all the data necessary to answer. Questions can also be 'open' in that learners are asked to use their own words, for example producing a list, a phrase, a sentence, a paragraph, a report.

EG Name three appliances that need a 13 amp fuse.

1.
2.
3.

A test might combine both 'closed' and 'open' questions, for example after identifying statements as true or false learners could be asked to explain their choices in their own words.

Visual

The learner can be asked to draw of complete a graph, or bar chart, or to label an illustration.

EG Write the correct colours alongside each of the wires to the 13 amp plug shown.

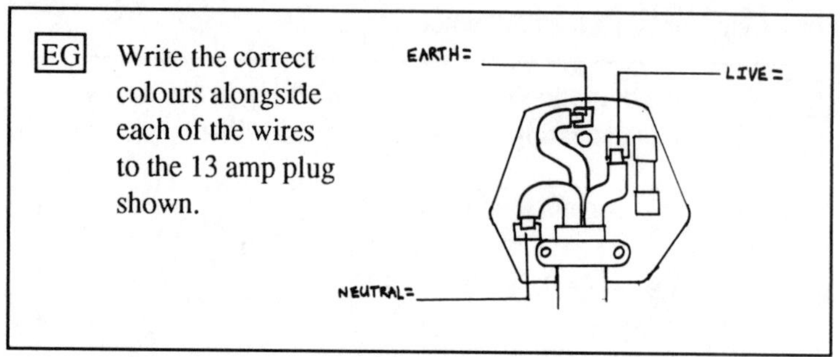

Numerical

The learner can be asked to complete a calculation or answer a series of questions involving the manipulation of numerical data.

EG There are 15,000 people living in Midtown. 750 own cars. What is the percentage of the population owning a car?

EG Look at Table X. By adding the columns in appropriate lines write down:

(1) the total number of people working in 1918
(2) the total number of men working in 1918
(3) the total number of women working in 1918.